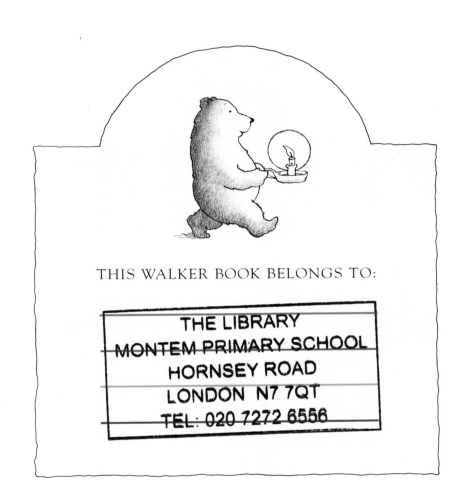

This book is about the builders of the pyramid of Senwosret I.
Senwosret was the son of Amenemhat I.
Senwosret built many monuments during his long reign.
He ruled Egypt from 1918 to 1875 BC.
His son Amenemhat II ruled from 1876 to 1842 BC.

Montuhotep was one of Senwosret's most important officials.
He served Senwosret as treasurer and was later
promoted to chief minister, overseeing the building and
completion of the pyramid.

We don't know the names of the other people who built the
pyramid; but the names used in the book have been taken from
people who lived at that time, doing these kinds of jobs.

The book is based on the published research
of Dieter and Dorothea Arnold of
The Metropolitan Museum of Art in New York.

Dr Richard Parkinson at the Department of Egyptian
Antiquities at the British Museum was the consultant.

For Rachel
M.H.

For Elliott & Cameron
R.H-B.

First published 2001 by Walker Books Ltd
87 Vauxhall Walk, London SE11 5HJ

This edition published 2002

2 4 6 8 10 9 7 5 3 1

Edited by Jackie Gaff, Camilla Hallinan and Paul Harrison
Designed by Beth Aves
Illustrations pages 32–36 Mike Bostock

This book has been typeset in Rusticana,
Myriad Tilt and Egyptienne

Printed in Hong Kong

British Library Cataloguing in Publication Data: a catalogue
record for this book is available from the British Library

ISBN 0-7445-8957-6

The land was given to me, its length and breadth; I have been nursed as a born conqueror. The land was given to me; I am its lord. My power has reached the heights of heaven △

A building text of Senwosret I, 1915 BC

WHO BUILT

THE PYRAMID?

by

MEREDITH HOOPER

illustrated by

**ROBIN
HEIGHWAY-BURY**

WALKER BOOKS
AND SUBSIDIARIES
LONDON • BOSTON • SYDNEY

With the lift of an eyebrow. With a word of command.

I am King of all Egypt. What I say happens.

My power reaches to the heights of heaven.

I built the pyramid as my tomb. After I die,

I shall lie beneath it, with my treasures around me.

My name will be remembered for all eternity.

I BUILT THE PYRAMID.

SAID MONTUHOTEP.

With my understanding of the king.

I am his Chief Minister.

Nothing happens without my knowing it.

Nothing is done without my ordering it.

I designed the pyramid so that

it would last for ever.

I decided where to hide His Majesty's

burial chamber, deep underground.

I do as my king wishes.

△

I BUILT THE PYRAMID.

I DID, SAID IMHOTEP.

With my secret knowledge

and my secret learning.

I am the High Priest of all Egypt.

It was I who chose where to build the pyramid.

It was I who calculated exactly

the direction it must face.

△

I BUILT THE PYRAMID.

I DID, SAID SENEBU.

With my experience,

thirty years of experience.

I'm the Quarry Master, the best in all Egypt.

I knew where to find the stones to build the pyramid.

Hard granite from far off in the desert.

Fine white limestone from across the Nile.

There's no pyramid without stones.

IT'S OBVIOUS.

I BUILT THE PYRAMID.

I DID, SAID AMENY.

With my know-how.

Me, Old Ameny, the Foreman of the gangs.

I knew how to hack through rock,

how to tunnel deep underground.

I cut out the place where His Majesty will lie

— life, prosperity, health to him!

Me, Old Ameny,

I BUILT THE PYRAMID.

With my muscles and sweat,

with blisters and aching bones.

Me and the other labourers.

We dragged the stones to the building site.

We pulled them up the ramps.

We pushed them into place on the pyramid.

WORK, WORK, WORK!

That's all I did.

I BUILT THE PYRAMID.

With my two tired legs.

With my two worn feet.

I'm the Water-carrier.

I carried water from a canal up to the building site.

Every day, in the hot sun, over the hot sand.

So many people needed water.

Without me, no one could get their work done.

Me and my donkey.

I BUILT THE PYRAMID.

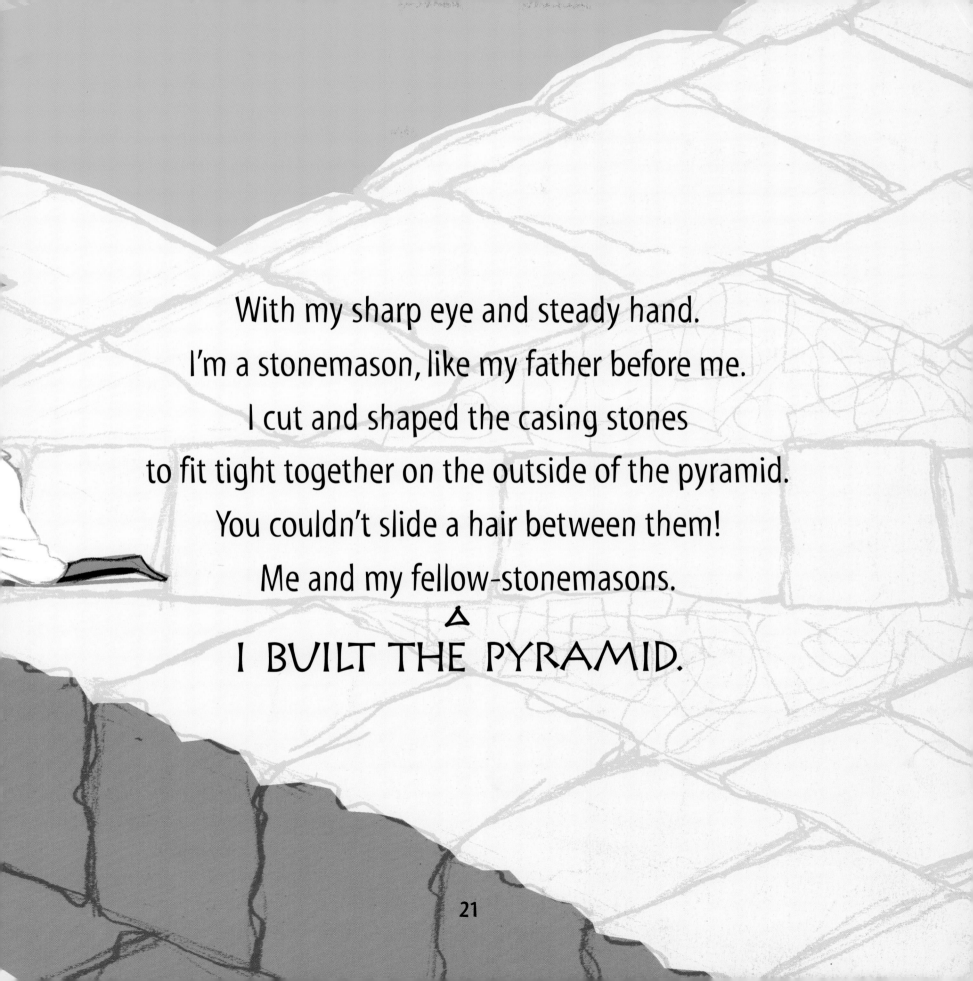

With my sharp eye and steady hand.

I'm a stonemason, like my father before me.

I cut and shaped the casing stones

to fit tight together on the outside of the pyramid.

You couldn't slide a hair between them!

Me and my fellow-stonemasons.

I BUILT THE PYRAMID.

I DID, SAID INYOTEF.

With my great talent,

my artistic gifts.

I am Inyotef the Sculptor.

It is I who carved the capstone.

The final stone, at the very top.

Without me

the pyramid was unfinished.

I decorated the capstone

with glittering gold,

and carved the pyramid's name:

"Senwosret Looks Over

the Two Lands".

△

I BUILT THE PYRAMID.

I DID, SAID

AMENEMHAT.

With the lift of an eyebrow.

With a word of command.

I am the new King of all Egypt.

I saw my father Senwosret's body

placed in his burial chamber. Then,

I ordered the burial chamber to be sealed,

for ever. I blocked the secret passage that led

to the burial chamber, and hid its entrance.

I completed the work.

△

I BUILT THE PYRAMID.

WHO BUILT THE

SAID SASOBEK.

Me and my tomb robbers,

we tunnelled down in the cramped airless dark.

Hard, sweaty, secret work.

We found the king's burial chamber.

We stole everything worth stealing.

All those others,

so what if they built the pyramid!

WE KNEW HOW
TO GET IN.

Deep under Senwosret's pyramid the robbers
in their cramped tunnel, wanted to get out, fast.
They dropped a few pieces of treasure in their hurry.
A golden dagger sheath. A few alabaster containers.
Bits of wooden boxes.

△

YEARS PASSED. Priests were
no longer living in the temple
buildings at the great pyramid.

Local people began
breaking into the site. They prised
off carvings and decorations, pulled
away the fine polished casing stones
covering the walls. They treated
the pyramid and its buildings as a
useful quarry.

The pyramid was sagging in any
case, sinking under its own weight.
Slowly the pyramid began to collapse.
Relentlessly the wind and weather
worked at the stones, wearing them,
bit by bit. Cracking them in the sun's
heat, the cold of the desert night.

Today Senwosret's pyramid is
a pile of sand and rubble just over a
third of its once great height.

Senwosret wanted his pyramid to last
for ever. It hasn't. It has decayed, like
everything else.

The pyramid of Senwosret I as it looks today.

The view from Senwosret's pyramid towards his father Amenemhat's pyramid, and the valley beyond.

THE FIRST archaeologists at the site of Senwosret's pyramid found the robbers' tunnel and the dropped pieces of treasure. They excavated the secret passage beneath the pyramid until near the bottom they were stopped by water. That was over 100 years ago.

Today, archaeologists working on the pyramid calculate that they have got within seven metres of Senwosret's burial chamber. But they cannot get through the final section of wet, sand-filled passage. Deep beneath the pyramid, the water level has been rising and the

burial chamber is now flooded.

Every burial chamber in every Egyptian pyramid was broken into by robbers. But Senwosret's burial chamber was robbed only once. No one has entered it since. No one today knows what the burial chamber looks like, or if anything remains inside.

A

RCHAEOLOGISTS from The Metropolitan Museum of Art in New York have found out a great deal about what Senwosret I's pyramid looked like, who built it and how. They sift through the heaps of rubble, the buried fragments, piecing together the evidence.

Stonemasons cut and smoothed the bottom and one side of each casing stone at the stone-dressing station.

This dotted line shows where the outer wall will be built.

Strong ramps built of brick, mud and rubble sloped up onto the pyramid itself.

This dotted line shows where the inner wall will be built.

Yard for storing granite, close to the entrance of the secret passage.

Storage yard for limestone quarried from nearby hills.

Blocks of stone were marked with information such as the name of the quarry, the dates of transport, route, when they were delivered to the storage area and when they were dragged to the pyramid.

Mud bricks made next to the Nile were stored here.

Good, wide roads were made of wooden beams buried in mortar and limestone chippings, sealed with Nile mud.

Brick buildings were used for site officials, workshops and to store tools, but we don't know their exact position.

Storage yard for Tura limestone.

Roads and ramps leading to local limestone quarries.

Archaeologists have not found the site of the royal city, nor the canal which would have led from the River Nile, but they were to the east of the pyramid.

The road leading down to the quay where the Tura limestone was unloaded as rough blocks.

CONSTRUCTION Site of SENWOSRET'S PYRAMID

10 20 30 40 50 60 70 80 90 100 110 120 130 140 150m

W
S — N
E

Granite was used for building the burial chamber, lining the secret passage and for the great plugs to block the passage.

The workmen's camp was probably in the valley between the pyramids of Senwosret and Amenemhat I.

Archaeologists are not sure exactly how the workmen lifted the stones over sixty metres up the side of the pyramid. Some of the stones weighed more than a tonne.

Road to the quay where granite was unloaded.

Archaeologists don't know exactly where the workshops of carpenters, metalworkers and potters were.

The COMPLETE PYRAMID Site

outer wall

inner wall

entrance chapel

temple for the king

ka-pyramid

causeway

Nine small pyramids were built, probably for Senwosret's queens, and a small ka-pyramid for Senwosret's spirit. There was an entrance chapel, a temple for the king, a causeway and another temple down in the valley. An inner wall with life-sized carved and painted figures of fat offering bearers surrounded the pyramid, with an outer wall beyond.

100m 200m

N

The site seen from above. Senwosret's pyramid left, Amenemhat's pyramid right.

SENWOSRET began to plan his pyramid as soon as he came to power. The pyramid of his father, Amenemhat I, was the first in Egypt for nearly 200 years. Amenemhat reunited Egypt and built a new capital city by the River Nile. Senwosret wanted his pyramid to be bigger and better than his father's. It was his royal tomb and he wanted it to last for ever.

Senwosret believed that after he died he would live again. But his new life depended on everything being done correctly when he died and afterwards. His body, with all the things he needed in his life after death, had to be kept safe so that his spirit could achieve new life, surrounded by his every requirement.

The pyramid of Senwosret I was built 4,000 years ago during the Middle Kingdom. Senwosret I ruled for forty-three years from 1918 to 1875 BC. This statue comes from the pyramid site and is now in the Egyptian Museum, Cairo.

△

MONTUHOTEP was Senwosret's Chief Minister. He was in charge of the royal architects who designed Senwosret's pyramid. He planned the work. He gave

PA Jürgen Liepe

A plan of the internal walls of the pyramid. The thirty-two spaces between the walls were filled with big slabs of roughly shaped stones.

the orders. The pyramid was to be built in a completely new way. A framework of huge, thick walls inside the pyramid would give it strength, like the skeleton in a body. There were no doors, passages or rooms. The king's body would lie safe, deep beneath a solid mountain of stone.

△

IMHOTEP, as High Priest, was in charge of the pyramid. Egyptians believed their king was a god, so the pyramid was also a temple. Imhotep chose a dramatic site for Senwosret's pyramid on a desert hilltop, close to his father's pyramid, beyond the royal city

In the great night sky, Imhotep could see a group of stars circling in the north, always visible. They were called the "Imperishable Ones". The secret passage, rising from the burial chamber like a pathway to the distant stars, had to face due north. So must Senwosret's burial chamber and coffin.

Imhotep laid out the huge square shape of the pyramid in the sand, facing exactly north, south, east and west.

Most of the stones needed to build the pyramid could be quarried nearby. But the limestone for the casing stones came from Tura, and the granite for the burial vault came from Aswan.

~~~~~~~~~~~~~~~~~~~~~~

Four deep foundation pits were dug, one in each corner of the pyramid square. Then Imhotep held a foundation ceremony. Priests put offerings in each pit – birds, animals, clay pots and bricks with the name of the pyramid. Now building could begin.

~~~~~~~~~~~~~~~~~~~~~~

Archaeologist's photograph of the offerings uncovered in one of the foundation pits.

GANGS of workmen dug a shaft in the centre of the pyramid square, hacking through solid limestone. A deep pit for the king's burial chamber was cut out of the rock at the bottom. Beyond the northern edge of the pyramid, more gangs dug a sloping ramp down towards the central shaft. Basket boys toiled up it, carrying away waste rock.

When the burial chamber was finished, the shaft and sloping tunnel were filled in and the ground levelled. A new, narrow, sloping passage was hacked through the rock, above the old construction tunnel: the secret entrance to the burial chamber. It would be used only once, to carry the king's body to his final resting place.

Perhaps 2,000 labourers worked on the construction site for two or four months at a time. Then they went back home to their villages to work in the fields again, while other labourers took their place.

Senwosret's pyramid was 61.25 metres high and each side was 105 metres long.

Shaft

Burial chamber

Secret entrance and passage

Construction tunnel

While the pyramid was being built its true shape could not be seen. It was hidden by ramps, roads, debris – all the mess of the construction site. But underneath, the four enormous triangular faces of Senwosret's pyramid had to rise with exactly the same slope, so that their tops came together, with no mistakes.

At the very top, a granite capstone was fitted into place, an exact miniature of the pyramid below. It was the only decorated stone on the whole pyramid. Eyes were carved on it as if Senwosret was looking out from inside, over his land.

Senwosret's capstone has not been found, but it probably looked like this capstone from the pyramid of Amenemhat III now in the Egyptian Museum, Cairo.

Werner Forman Archive, Egyptian Museum, Cairo

Now stonemasons started at the top of the pyramid, working down. The fine Tura limestone casing stones covering the pyramid's sides fitted tightly together. But their fronts had been left bulging, unfinished. The stonemasons cut away the spare stone, chiselling and polishing, rubbing the angled surfaces with grinding stones and sand.

The true pyramid began to glare and shine.

Senwosret's pyramid was the biggest and highest built in Egypt for 500 years. Perhaps 5,000 quarrymen, masons, labourers and other workmen – specialists, as well as support staff – were needed to build it.

An enormous amount of material was used: thousands of basket-loads of sand from the desert; thousands of moulds filled with Nile mud, to make bricks; thousands of trees to make tools, sledges, boats, to burn for fuel, to cook food; tens of thousands of jars of water; around a quarter of a million stones – limestone and granite, alabaster, dolerite and quartzite; continuous supplies for meals – bread and beer, vegetables and fish.

Building the pyramid was a massive task. It happened because of the countless repetition of jobs, by vast numbers of people. The pyramid of Senwosret I looked magnificent when it was finished. It probably took twenty years to build.

SON OF THE SUN GOD: SENWOSRET, MAY HE LIVE FOR ALL TIME AND ETERNITY.

Index

The high inner wall enclosing the pyramid was decorated in unique style on both sides with carved and painted panels. Two long processions of life-size offering bearers move around the pyramid ending at the temple of the king, Senwosret I.

MEREDITH HOOPER

uses the storybook form in
Who Built the Pyramid? to bring
the latest research to a wider
audience. A historian by training,
she enjoys working closely
with subject specialists.
Her many titles range from
Antarctica to aviation,
from the history of water to
the history of inventions.

A much travelled Australian, she
lives with her family in London.

ROBIN
HEIGHWAY-BURY

has been illustrating for
sixteen years, but this is his
first book for children.
Robin lives in London and
found inspiration
for his paintings from
the Egyptian galleries of
the British Museum,
which was very
close to his studio.